CurriculumVisions 2E Science@School

Royal Borough of Kingston Upon Thames

Forces and movement

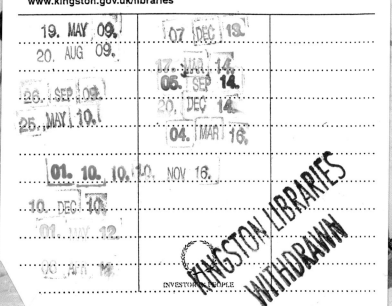
Pete ... pp

Curriculum Visions

Science@School

Teacher's Guide
There is a Teacher's Guide available
to accompany this book.

Dedicated Web Site
There is a wealth of supporting
material including videos and activities
available at the Professional Zone,
part of our dedicated web site:

www.CurriculumVisions.com

The Professional Zone
is a subscription zone.

A CVP Book.
First published in 2008

Copyright © 2008 Earthscape

Authors
Peter Riley, BSc, C Biol, MI Biol, PGCE,
and Brian Knapp, BSc, PhD

Senior Designer
Adele Humphries, BA, PGCE

Educational Consultant
Jan Smith (former Deputy Head of Wellfield School,
Burnley, Lancashire)

Editor
Gillian Gatehouse

Designed and produced by
EARTHSCAPE

Printed in China by
WKT Co., Ltd

Curriculum Visions Science@School
Volume 2E Forces and movement
A CIP record for this book is available
from the British Library.

ISBN: 978 1 86214 263 3

Picture credits
All pictures are from the Earthscape and
ShutterStock collections.

As an athlete pulls on her pole,
it nearly bends right over.

 # Contents

Weblink: www.curriculumvisions.com

Ways of moving

There are many ways of moving.

Look around you. Most things are still. They don't move. But we move, animals move, aeroplanes and cars move. So why do some things move while others stay still?

The answer is that something has to get them going. They have to be pushed or pulled. An aeroplane or a car are pushed by their engines. Animals move using their muscles.

An aeroplane flies through the air using its engines.

A ballet dancer jumps high in the air using muscles in her legs.

A boy races around
a go-kart track.
The go-kart is pushed
along by its engine.

A horse jumps over a fence by
using the muscles in its legs.

A hummingbird hovers in
the air by beating its wings
up and down very quickly.

What other ways of moving can you think of?

Weblink: www.curriculumvisions.com

Changing shape

You can change the shapes of some objects when you push or pull them.

When you push most things they move away from you. But if you hold soft things, springy things, or bendy things tightly, they change shape instead.

You can see the way things change shape on this page.

A potter uses a wheel to turn the soft clay. Then he PUSHES on it with his fingers and it begins to change shape.

He can PUSH with his fingers to make grooves.

He can PULL with his hand to draw the clay up into a vase shape.
He can then PUSH on the edge with a scraper to get a smooth finish.

When you squeeze a sponge you PUSH your fingers together and the sponge changes shape.

An athlete pulls on one end of a pole and it bends.

To make a rubber band get longer you pull it.

When you blow a bubble you push on the soap film and stretch it.

Do you pull or push on clay to roll it into a ball?

Weblink: www.curriculumvisions.com

Gravity

3

The Earth pulls on everything. This pull is called gravity.

The most common pull in the world is all around you. You can't see it, but once you know it is there, you can see how important it is. The pull is caused by the Earth and it is called gravity.

If you throw a ball high into the air, gravity pulls it back. If you trip up, gravity makes you fall to the ground. You don't float off into space because of gravity.

If you go up, like walking up a mountain, you have to work hard against gravity. If you go down, like skiing, gravity gives you a helping hand.

When you pour milk onto your breakfast, it always goes downwards. This is the effect of gravity.

Weblink: www.curriculumvisions.com

This climber is finding it hard to climb because he is having to work against gravity.

If you sit at the top of a slide you will always slide down.

You use gravity just to do simple things like comb your hair. This is an astronaut in space trying to comb her hair! There is no gravity on the Space Station.

Why do you think you can fall down a hole?

Weblink: www.curriculumvisions.com

4

On the move

A push or pull changes how things move.

If you push or pull something you make it move in the same direction as the push or pull.

So how do you make something turn? You can pull or push it from the sides, but there is a better way. Cars, bikes and scooters all have front wheels that can be turned in the way you want to go. A boat has a rudder so it can be turned, too.

This girl is moving because she is being pushed by her grandfather. She is moving in the same direction that her grandfather is pushing.

A train is pulled along by its engine.

A car changes direction when the driver turns the wheels.

The yacht is moved by the force of the wind. It changes direction by using a rudder.

What happens to the train when the engine stops pulling?

Weblink: www.curriculumvisions.com

5 Going faster

We can make ourselves move faster. This is called acceleration.

If you want to go faster, you have to put in more effort, that is more push or more pull. To run faster you can take more steps a minute. You can also take more powerful steps. Of course, you can also do both at the same time.

Racing cyclists go faster by pushing harder on the pedals and so peddling more times a minute.

Swimmers push harder against the water and try to do more strokes to the minute.

You can make a rowing boat travel faster by moving the oars more quickly.

How do you win a sack race?

6 Friction

Most surfaces have grip. It stops you sliding about. A scientist's word for grip is friction.

Just imagine what it would be like if things didn't grip! You would fall over each time you moved and then you would go sliding into a wall.

The grip that helps to make our world work is called friction. It's another important force like gravity. Gravity makes things move; friction helps to stop things moving.

You can make friction less by polishing a surface. You can make friction more by roughening a surface. You can see examples here.

CAUTION WET FLOOR

If there is a liquid, like water, between two surfaces, then friction is lower. So when the floor is wet there is less grip and people can slip and fall.

Weblink: www.curriculumvisions.com

A snowboarder polishes the underside of the board so that it will slip over the snow more easily.

When two objects scrape against one another, heat can be made. This is how matches work.

This snow-clearing machine has chains on its tyres to give it better grip.

If you slide your foot over different floor surfaces, does it feel as though friction is always the same?

15

7 Going slower

You will go slower if you stop
using a pushing or pulling force.

If you want to go slower you use friction.
Friction will slow you down and bring you
to a stop quickly or slowly.

If you stop pulling or pushing, friction
will gradually bring you to a stop.
You can slow down more quickly by
making friction bigger. This is what
happens when you put on the brakes
on your bike or grip the sides of a slide.

Weblink: www.curriculumvisions.com

You can slow down on roller blades if you do not move your legs.

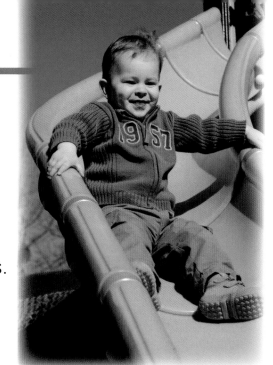

You can move more slowly down a slide if you grip its sides.

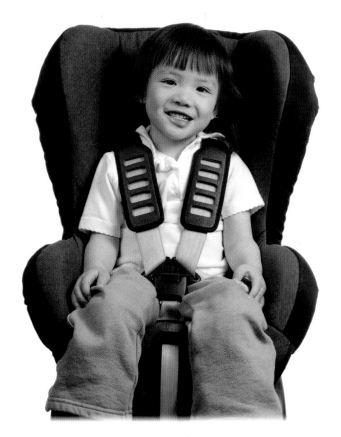

You slow down quickly when you put on the brakes.

Friction is not enough to keep you in your seat when a car slows down very quickly. You need a safety belt.

How do you slow a rowing boat down?

Weblink: www.curriculumvisions.com

Toy cars

You can investigate moving, going faster and going slower with a toy car.

Do an investigation

Prop one end of a board up using wooden blocks. This gives you a slope called a ramp.

1. Place the car at the top of the ramp. Then let it go. It will rush down the ramp and travel across your tabletop.

2. Now measure how far it moves before it comes to a stop.

3. Put some more blocks under the board to make the ramp steeper. Repeat your experiment and measure how far the car moved before it came to a stop.

4. Now take most of the blocks away. What do you think will happen? Repeat your experiment to see if you are right.

Weblink: www.curriculumvisions.com

1 Place the car at the top of the ramp.

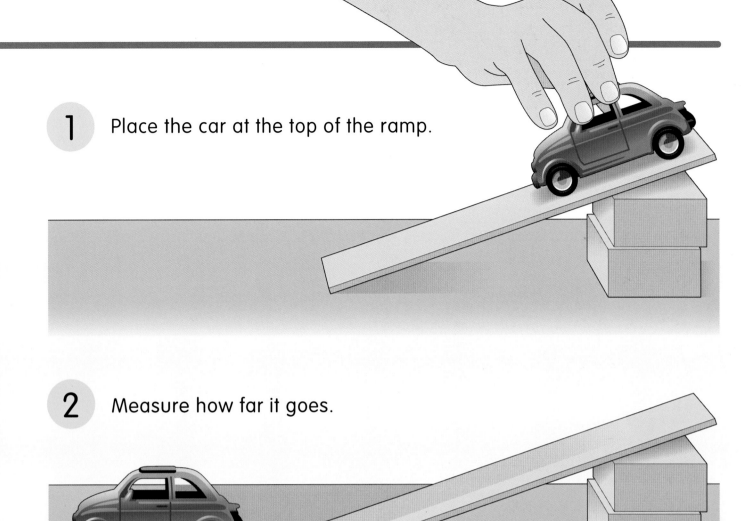

2 Measure how far it goes.

How does it work?

The car is pulled down the ramp by gravity. Gravity is more powerful than friction. When the car goes on the flat surface, gravity stops pulling it forwards. Friction then makes the car stop.

What would happen to the cars if you covered the table with a tablecloth?

Weblink: www.curriculumvisions.com

Weight

The pulling force of gravity gives everything weight.

Force is the word scientists use for a push or a pull. Weight is the everyday word we use for a force that pulls things down. When you hold something, you might say 'this is heavy', or 'this is light', or 'it weighs a lot'.

The object is being pulled down by gravity. It's pulling down on your hand which is how you can tell if it is light or heavy.

This is a kilo weight used on some food scales.

There are spring scales to measure your weight, and the weight of food.

Weblink: www.curriculumvisions.com

Do an investigation

You can measure the weight of things using a spring scale.

1 You need a flowerpot saucer and some string to make the pan. You need a ruler, a strong elastic band and a bent paperclip to be a hook and a pointer.

2 Add small objects to the pan and see how far down the scale the pointer moves.

Before you add each object try to guess if it will weigh more or less than the one before it.

Take care when using elastic bands and pointers. You may want to wear eye protection.

elastic band

hook

pointer

ruler

pan

Make this spring scale to measure the force called weight for a variety of objects around you.

Words to learn

Astronaut

A person who lives and works in space.

Athlete

A person who takes part in sports such as swimming, running, jumping and throwing.

Brake

The part of a bicycle next to the wheels that makes the bicycle stop. Brakes work by making a strong friction force.

Friction

The grip between two things that are touching. Lots of friction can make things hot.

Weblink: www.curriculumvisions.com

Gravity

The pulling force of the Earth.

Ramp

A slope.

Rudder

An upright piece of wood or metal at the back of the boat which is turned in the water to steer.

rudder

Scales

A simple machine for weighing things.

Weight

The everyday word we use for a force that pulls things down.

Weblink: www.curriculumvisions.com

Index

Weblink: www.curriculumvisions.com